THE CRYSTALS JOURNAL

INCORPORATE THE POWER OF
CRYSTALS INTO YOUR LIFE

QUINN BOULEY

PETER PAUPER PRESS, INC.
WHITE PLAINS, NEW YORK

PETER PAUPER PRESS
Fine Books and Gifts Since 1928

OUR COMPANY

In 1928, at the age of twenty-two, Peter Beilenson began printing books on a small press in the basement of his parents' home in Larchmont, New York. Peter—and later, his wife, Edna—sought to create fine books that sold at "prices even a pauper could afford."

Today, still family owned and operated, Peter Pauper Press continues to honor our founders' legacy—and our customers' expectations—of beauty, quality, and value.

To my husband Roger, who never questions my crazy ideas and encourages me every step of the way to go for it. You are my living guardian angel.

Designed by Margaret Rubiano

Images used under license from Shutterstock.com

Text copyright © 2021 Quinn Bouley
Peter Pauper Press, Inc.
202 Mamaroneck Avenue
White Plains, NY 10601 USA
All rights reserved
ISBN 978-1-4413-3580-7
Printed in China
7 6 5 4 3 2 1

Visit us at www.peterpauper.com

THE CRYSTALS JOURNAL

INCORPORATE THE POWER OF CRYSTALS INTO YOUR LIFE

QUINN BOULEY

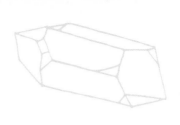

CONTENTS

PREFACE 6

PART I–THE LOW DOWN ON CRYSTALS 8

CRYSTAL CARE 9

Choosing a Crystal 9

Clear and Charge Your Crystals 9

Program and Activate Your Crystals 11

Crystal Maintenance 11

INCORPORATE CRYSTALS INTO YOUR LIFE 14

Crystals in the Home and Office 14

Wearing and Carrying Crystals 14

Talismans 15

Meditating with Crystals 16

Crystals and Magic 17

Record Your Crystal Charms and Spells 17

Home Protection Jar 22

HEALING WITH CRYSTALS 24

Chakra Balancing Layout 25

Record Your Crystal Healing Layouts 26

CRYSTAL ESSENCE 36

Remedies for Anxiety, Cleansing, or Recharging 39

Record Your Gem Essence Recipes 40

CRYSTAL GRIDS 46

Record Your Crystal Grids 49

CRYSTAL CORRESPONDENCES 54

    Crystals and Chakras 54

    Crystals and the Zodiac 56

    Internal Crystal Structures 58

    External Crystal Structures 60

    Color Energies and Crystals 62

    Moon Phases and Crystals 63

MINI CRYSTALPEDIA 64

PART II—THE JOURNAL 81

USING THE JOURNAL 82

CRYSTAL JOURNAL PAGES 84

CRYSTAL WISH LIST 186

RESOURCES 188

NOTES 191

ABOUT THE AUTHOR 192

PREFACE

My name is Quinn, and I'm addicted to crystals. Who could blame me, really? The way they dazzle and twinkle has me completely hypnotized. Then there is the perfection of their inner crystalline structure, which fascinates me for hours and leads me to contemplate the origins of life. Let me not forget the unique rainbow of frequencies each crystal emits, drawing me into its harmonic embrace. How could I resist welcoming these enchanted beauties of the mineral kingdom into my life every chance I get? For me, crystals are much more than decorative objects. They are living extensions of Earth that hold the memory and energy of all that has passed since the planet began to form. Crystals are my allies in my life's journey, helping me reach wholeness in my mind, body, and spirit, and aligning me with the universal flow. I invite you to explore the world of crystals and how they can enhance your life.

I could go on for days about the science associated with crystals, but I'm going to do you a solid and keep things simple. Crystals are substances whose particles are arranged in a repeating geometric pattern that forms the three dimensional crystal structure. Earth began forming crystals billions of years ago. Crystals can take shape in a number of ways, such as when water evaporates from a chemical mixture; when water contains more dissolved minerals than it can hold; or when lava cools and hardens. The speed of the process, temperature, and pressure deep beneath the planet's surface affect how the crystal turns out. There are seriously thousands of types of crystals, and many yet to be discovered. As the Earth changes, it may create new and different crystalline structures.

Humans enhance crystals found in nature, and have also created synthetic and imitation crystals. We cut and polish natural stones, and even treat them with radiation or heat to enhance their color. A synthetic crystal is made in a lab but has the same physical and chemical makeup as its Earth-made equivalent.

An imitation stone is created using materials like resin glass and plastics to look like a crystal, but doesn't actually have a crystalline structure. Telling the difference is not always easy, but responsible sellers will have no problem sharing this info with you, so don't be afraid to ask questions.

Now that you understand the physical properties of these crystals, let's chat about their energetic properties. They may look like solid inanimate objects, but like everything else in the world, each crystal is made up of atoms that vibrate at a certain frequency. We tap into these frequencies using our own subtle energy field *We tap into these frequencies using our own subtle energy field to understand and use a crystal's unique gifts.* to understand and use a crystal's unique gifts. Science may not be focused on proving the existence of crystals' energetic properties and how they affect our lives. Scientists are, however, discovering more about using certain crystals to conduct and generate energy with piezoelectricity and pyroelectricity. (For my true nerd friends: Google these terms and be amazed.) I personally don't need science to tell me my divine intuition is right, because I feel the truth resonates with my soul. I think we often forget that we are creatures of this Earth, formed from the same stardust as the rest of the universe. Working with the energy of crystals feels very natural to me.

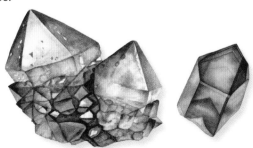

PART 1

THE
LOW DOWN
ON CRYSTALS

CRYSTAL CARE

CHOOSING A CRYSTAL

THERE IS NOTHING MORE EXCITING FOR ME THAN WALKING INTO MY LOCAL CRYSTAL SHOP and exploring every inch to find my next crystal. Seeing hundreds of different crystals in an array of cuts and sizes can also feel totally overwhelming, making it hard to know where to begin. There are a few simple ways to navigate this mind-blowing feeling and find the crystal that is right for you. First, if you have a specific purpose, do some research before you go and make a list of possible stones that would work with your needs. This will help to narrow things down. Then let your intuition guide you to the stone that's right for you. Sometimes when a stone is right for me it will feel warm in my hand or make my hand tingle, but most of the time it just feels right. Another option when you enter a shop is to take a few deep breaths to relax yourself, then ask the universe to show you the one that is right for you. There is no wrong way to choose.

CLEAR AND CHARGE YOUR CRYSTALS

Cleansing and charging your crystals is a very important step when you first get a crystal, but also as ongoing crystal maintenance. Clearing or cleansing resets your crystal by removing previously stored energies from other people or places. Charging crystals restores their power and reinforces our connection with them. It's like plugging them in to power up. You only need one technique to get your crystal in good working order, but I like to combine several techniques and make a ritual out of it. I call it giving my crystals a spa day.

> *Charging crystals restores their power and reinforces our connection with them.*

It is always best to charge crystals in a relaxed, meditative state. Here are some methods you can try:

1. **WATER:** Soak your crystal in water or salt water for several hours, rinse them in a stream or other body of water, or set them out in the rain. Just make sure beforehand that water won't break your crystals down. (See page 12.)

2. **SEA SALT:** Place crystals gently on top of a layer of sea salt. If you are worried about the salt breaking them down or scratching them, place an organic piece of cotton on top of the salt, then lay out your crystals. I prefer the fabric to be undyed or dyed only with natural plant dyes.

3. **SOUND BATH:** Use singing bowls or tuning forks for 3 to 5 minutes.

4. **SACRED SMOKE:** Take cleansing herbs, bundle them together, and burn them. Then pass the crystals through the smoke.

5. **SPRAYS:** Make or buy sprays for crystal clearing.

6. **REIKI:** If you are trained in Reiki or other energy healing techniques, then by all means clear your crystals that way.

7. **SUN:** Place your crystals in direct sunlight for a minimum of 3 hours. First, though, do your research to make sure your crystal won't crack, become brittle, or fade in sunlight. (See page 13.)

8. **MOON:** Place your crystal in direct moonlight after the sun sets, then retrieve it before the sun comes up. Take into account how each phase of the moon will influence the crystal's energy.

9. **EARTH:** Bury your crystals in the ground for at least 24 hours. In winter, the ground is frozen where I live, so I like to keep a large pot of dirt handy that I can place my crystals in.

You know the theory that houseplants grow better and faster when you talk to them? Well, I have also found that my crystals enjoy attention. They seem to thrive when I interact with them.

Once your crystal is cleared and charged, you can store it or move on to programming it.

PROGRAM AND ACTIVATE YOUR CRYSTALS

In this step, you dedicate your crystal to a specific purpose. Think of it as a way of communicating with your crystal and building your relationship.

Before you begin, spend a few minutes taking slow deep breaths and centering yourself. Let go of stray thoughts as your mind becomes still.

Hold your crystal in your hand and tell it what you wish to accomplish. Maybe it's love, abundance, healing, or something else. You can communicate using spontaneous heartfelt words, a specific intention or affirmation, mantras or chants, visualization, or meditation. Let your intuition guide you. After all, this is a very personal relationship and only you can decide the best way to connect with your crystal. If your purpose for this crystal has a long-term goal, you may consider recharging it once a week or once a month, depending on use.

CRYSTAL MAINTENANCE

Once you have finished working with a crystal for a given intention, simply thank it for its service and follow your clearing and charging directions. There may also come a time when a crystal cracks, chips, or shatters, and you will need to choose what the crystal is communicating to you. If you decide to continue your work with the crystal, I suggest giving it a break, as well as a deep cleaning using several techniques above. If you decide it is time to move on from that crystal, I suggest burying it back in the earth from where it came.

CRYSTALS **NOT** TO SOAK IN WATER

The following is a partial list of common crystals that may dissolve or break apart when soaked in water.

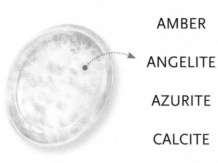

AMBER	MALACHITE
ANGELITE	MOLDAVITE
AZURITE	MOONSTONE
CALCITE	OBSIDIAN
CARNELIAN	OPAL
CELESTITE	PYRITE
FLUORITE	RHODOCHROSITE
KYANITE	SELENITE
LABRADORITE	SPIRIT QUARTZ
LEPIDOLITE	TURQUOISE

CRYSTALS TO KEEP OUT OF THE SUN

The following is a partial list of common crystals that may fade, become brittle, or crack in sunlight.

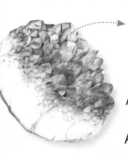

 AMETHYST

APATITE

APOPHYLLITE

AQUAMARINE

 AVENTURINE

BERYL

CHRYSOCOLLA

CITRINE

FLUORITE

KUNZITE

ROSE QUARTZ

SAPPHIRE

SMOKY QUARTZ

SPIRIT QUARTZ

SUPER SEVEN

INCORPORATE CRYSTALS INTO YOUR LIFE

CHOOSING CRYSTALS TO ENHANCE YOUR LIFE CAN BE REALLY FUN AND CREATIVE. Just let your intuition guide you in determining which practices may benefit you. No need to be rigid. As for which crystals to choose for which purposes, use the Mini Crystalpedia section that begins on page 64 for guidance. Have fun and explore one or all the techniques.

CRYSTALS IN THE HOME AND OFFICE

Crystals make absolutely stunning décor, but they also add tons of good vibes to a space. Placing them in your sacred spot to assist you in your spiritual journey is a wonderful way to start, but feel free to scatter them throughout your space. In my home, I place them in my plants. The crystals lend their energy to the plant's health and growth, or can amplify the effects of that plant on my environment. My other favorite spots include: near doors for home protection, under or next to my bed for restful sleep, and near my electronic devices to absorb damaging electromagnetic

Certain stones can give us confidence for a big event or provide focus and clarity before a test.

fields. Don't forget to fill your office with crystals, too. They can be useful for increasing productivity, promoting workplace harmony, and furthering success.

WEARING AND CARRYING CRYSTALS

Adorning our bodies with crystals has been an obsession for centuries in cultures around the world. Sure, they make stunning eye candy, but they can also be worn or carried to manifest an array of desires. Wear them to attract love, protect yourself from all kinds of negative mojo, or calm anxiety. Certain stones can give us confidence for a big event or provide focus and clarity before a test. The uses are only limited by your imagination.

TALISMANS

A talisman is a natural object charged with a specific intention and kept close to the body by wearing it as jewelry or carrying it in a pocket. It is an awesome way to turn your bling into a powerful device to manifest anything you desire.

To make your own talisman, begin by deciding what you wish to manifest, and choosing a crystal or piece of jewelry to amplify your intention. Select a stone that corresponds with your aims.

- Take several deep breaths and let your thoughts go. Once you feel calm and still, move on to the next step.

- Clear yourself and your chosen piece using sacred smoke or a crystal cleanse spray. (See page 39.)

- Hold the talisman in your hand and state your intention in your mind or aloud.

- *"May this talisman . . ."* (Spontaneously describe how this talisman will assist you in manifesting your desire.)

- Now put your talisman on.

- Spend a few minutes visualizing your intention as if it has already happened.

- Give thanks in your mind or aloud for what you will receive. Really feel it, knowing in your heart that it is already manifest.

- Slowly begin to come back. Feel the earth beneath you.

- Recharge your talisman once a month under the light of the full moon.

MEDITATING WITH CRYSTALS

Don't even get me started on the crazy awesome benefits of meditation by itself. Add crystals, and boom: It's a whole new level of badassery. They are a fantastic aid in reaching higher levels of consciousness. Crystals like quartz are amazingly helpful if you are a newbie meditator and are having a hard time focusing or relaxing. Meditating with a new crystal is also a great way to get to know its unique energy frequency and build your relationship with that crystal. Are you in need of a specific energy? Then grab an appropriate stone, set your intention, and meditate.

CRYSTALS AND MAGIC

Use the energy of crystals in your magical work with **charms**, **spells**, and **rituals**. Crystals in spells and charms work much like candles, oils, and herbs, but they also have the benefit of amplifying energetic properties. They are super easy to incorporate. Just choose crystals that work in harmony with your purpose.

RECORD YOUR CRYSTAL CHARMS AND SPELLS

Name: _____

Intent: _____

Ingredients:

_____   _____

_____   _____

_____   _____

_____   _____

_____   _____

_____   _____

_____   _____

Timing: _____

Instructions/Notes:

_____

_____

_____

_____

_____

CRYSTAL CHARMS AND SPELLS

Name: _____

Intent: _____

Ingredients:

_____	_____
_____	_____
_____	_____
_____	_____
_____	_____
_____	_____
_____	_____

Timing: _____

Instructions/Notes:

_____

_____

_____

_____

_____

_____

_____

_____

Name: _____

Intent: _____

Ingredients:

_____   _____

_____   _____

_____   _____

_____   _____

_____   _____

_____   _____

_____   _____

Timing: _____

Instructions/Notes:

_____

_____

_____

_____

_____

_____

_____

_____

_____

CRYSTAL CHARMS AND SPELLS

Name: _____

Intent: _____

Ingredients:

_____   _____

_____   _____

_____   _____

_____   _____

_____   _____

_____   _____

_____   _____

Timing: _____

Instructions/Notes:

_____

_____

_____

_____

_____

_____

_____

_____

Name: _____

Intent: _____

Ingredients:

_____   _____

_____   _____

_____   _____

_____   _____

_____   _____

_____   _____

_____   _____

Timing: _____

Instructions/Notes:

_____

_____

_____

_____

_____

_____

_____

_____

_____

_____

LEAVE NEGATIVITY AT THE DOOR: HOME PROTECTION JAR

This jar is perfect to protect your home and transmute any negative energy that may enter.

SUPPLIES:

Sea salt

Mason jar or other
glass jar with cover

Dried basil

Dried bay leaves

Cleansed and charged
black tourmaline

Cleansed and charged
amethyst

- Find a quiet, peaceful place where you will not be disturbed.

- Take a few deep breaths and relax. Release thoughts and let your mind still.

- Use a spray or sacred smoke to cleanse yourself and the supplies.

- Say the intention in your mind or aloud.

  May the elements placed in this jar lend their energy to protect this home and repel negativity. May this protective energy radiate and enclose our entire home and all that dwell within it. May it transform negative energy or intentions into love and positivity.

- Take your jar and place all your supplies within it and put the cover on.

- Hold your jar and visualize your home that is safe and happy. Don't just see it, but *feel* what a safe, positive, happy home is like. The more senses you incorporate, the more powerful the energy you create.

- Then chant the following over and over while holding the jar until you feel the energy from your chant build and release. Let your intuition tell you when it has been released. Don't worry if you are not sure when to stop. You can't do it wrong. The more you begin to trust your intuition, the easier it will become.

"My home and all within it
are safe and protected."

- Give deeply felt thanks for the blessing of having a safe and protected home.

- Ground yourself and come back slowly. Feel the earth beneath you.

- Place the jar you created near the door people use most often to enter your home.

BAY

BLACK
TOURMALINE

BASIL

AMETHYST

HEALING WITH CRYSTALS

First, a disclaimer: It's important to note that crystal healing is a supplement to, not a substitute for, medical care. If you're not well, always seek medical care first and foremost. Crystals may aid in your holistic well-being, but they can't be solely relied upon to cure ailments or injuries.

That said, crystal healing is an amazing complementary healing modality, but there are many misconceptions about how to effectively use crystals for healing. The biggest misunderstanding may be that someone goes out and grabs a specific stone for a specific ailment they have, and thinks the crystal will heal them. When this isn't the case, they think they did it wrong, or crystal healing doesn't actually work. Let's clear up why this method is ineffective.

First: Crystal healing works on the whole being by restoring balance. Through this balance, we manifest the healing of physical, mental, emotional, or spiritual ailments. So using a guided-missile approach to your ailment won't be as effective as looking at the whole picture of your health.

Second: Crystals are a tool, and like all tools, they need someone to use them in order for them to work. For example, a vacuum is a great tool for cleaning your home, but it won't be very helpful if you just buy one, bring it home, and expect it to clean your floors. In order for the vacuum to work, you need to plug it in, turn it on, and move it across the surface of the floor.

Crystals are very much the same way. It is important to interact with them in some of the ways described in this book in order for them to aid you. As you work with them, you will begin to see a beautiful co-creative relationship grow.

Crystals offer healing energy to us with their unique vibrational frequency through a process of resonance, which is when the vibration of the crystal synchronizes with your vibrations and harmonizes them, removing discord.

CHAKRA BALANCING LAYOUT

This is a simple layout that targets restoring your body to wholeness through the placement of crystals on the body's energy centers, called **chakras**. Feel free to switch out any stone for one that you are intuitively drawn to. When doing crystal healing, listen to your intuition above all else. *(See pages 54-55 for crystal and chakra correspondences.)*

1. GATHER YOUR CRYSTALS. They should be cleared and charged.

2. OPTIONAL: Cleanse yourself and your space using sacred smoke or clearing spray.

3. LAY ON A COMFORTABLE SURFACE WITH THE STONES in your hand. Take several deep cleansing breaths until you feel your mind settle and you are present in the moment.

4. SET A HEALING INTENTION FOR THE STONES. Let your intuition guide you. I speak to my crystals as if they're good friends I'm asking to help me out.

5. PLACE EACH STONE ON THE CORRESPONDING CHAKRA. You may wish to speak again to each stone individually as you place it, or maybe just thank it for being here with you.

6. LAY IN MEDITATION FOR 20 MINUTES or until your intuition has signaled that the healing is complete. You may feel all kinds of sensations, and some may even be unpleasant, but they will not hurt you. Simply try to relax and be interested in the energy as it moves through you. Don't judge what happens. You do not need to do a thing. You may feel nothing except relaxed, or the same as before, and that is okay too.

7. SAY WORDS OF THANKS and remove your crystals. Move slowly before standing up.

8. REPEAT WHENEVER YOU LIKE.

Name: _____

Lapiz Lazuli

Adventurine

Carnelian

Amethyst

Tourquoise

Tigers eye

Red jasper

ON LINES ABOVE,
WRITE WHICH
CRYSTAL YOU USE
FOR EACH CHAKRA.

Purpose Notes:

_____

_____

_____

_____

_____

_____

CHAKRA BALANCING LAYOUTS

Name: _____

Purpose Notes:

_____

_____

_____

_____

_____

_____

_____

Name: _____

Purpose Notes:

_____

_____

_____

_____

_____

_____

Name: _____

Purpose Notes:

_____

_____

_____

_____

_____

_____

Name: _____

Purpose Notes:

_____

_____

_____

_____

_____

_____

_____

Name: _____

Purpose Notes:

_____

_____

_____

_____

_____

_____

_____

Name: _____

Purpose Notes:

_____

_____

_____

_____

_____

_____

_____

CHAKRA BALANCING LAYOUTS

Name: _____

Purpose Notes:

_____

_____

_____

_____

_____

_____

_____

Name: _____

Purpose Notes:

_____

_____

_____

_____

_____

_____

_____

CHAKRA BALANCING LAYOUTS

Name: _____

Purpose Notes:

_____

_____

_____

_____

_____

_____

_____

CRYSTAL ESSENCE

Crystal essence is a way of infusing water or carrier oil with the vibrations of a crystal or group of crystals. Crystal essences can then be used in a variety of cool ways. If safe to do so, they can be taken internally as therapeutic drops, or added to your drinking water. Use their properties for beauty care in skin and hair treatments or body oils. You can also make yourself some sprays for clearing, grounding, protection, and so on. You can choose one crystal or combine several to achieve specific results.

There are two ways to make crystal essence: the direct and indirect method.

CRYSTAL ESSENCE
DIRECT METHOD

I don't recommend the direct method unless you're a highly trained professional. If you do not have extensive knowledge of crystals, using this method could pose a significant problem because some crystals contain materials that are toxic if ingested, like lead or mercury, while others can't be soaked because it will break down their structure. In the direct method, crystals are soaked directly in a container with water or oil and placed in the sunlight or moonlight for a few hours to be infused. However, there is another method, and it is super easy and just as effective. The indirect method is performed the same way as the direct method, except the crystals are placed in a separate glass container that is then submerged into the liquid.

CRYSTAL ESSENCE
INDIRECT METHOD

SUPPLIES:

- Your choice of crystal or combination of crystals, cleared and charged

- 2 glass containers, one that holds at least 8 oz. of water, and one small enough to fit inside the first while holding the crystals (Containers should be sterile and have lids or coverings.)

- Distilled or spring water, or a carrier oil such as jojoba, sweet almond, or grapeseed

- Dark glass bottles or containers to hold your essence after it's made (Bottles should also be sterile.)

- Labels for containers

- Vodka, optional
  (You only need vodka if you want your essence to last more than a few days. Oil essence doesn't need a preservative, and neither does water consumed right away.)

- Funnel, to transfer essence to smaller bottles (optional)

DIRECTIONS:

- Take a few deep breaths to center yourself and calm your mind.

- Set a simple intention or affirmation for your crystal essence.

- Take the smaller of your two glass containers, place your crystals inside, and cover tightly. You do not want any liquid to enter this container. Then place the smaller jar into the larger glass container. Fill the large container with 8 ounces of water or oil and cover.

- Place your containers in direct sunlight or moonlight. For sunlight, I

CONTINUED ON NEXT PAGE

like to leave it for six to eight hours, and when I'm using moonlight, two consecutive nights. I place the container outside when the sun sets, and in the morning I bring it inside to a quiet place so it won't be touched or disturbed. In the evening I repeat.

- When complete, gather your containers, remove the smaller jar of crystals, and say words of thanks.

- If you used water to make your essence, go ahead and drink it straight or store it in the fridge for up to 48 hours.

- If you want to preserve your crystal essence, make a crystal remedy by filling a sterile dark glass container with half vodka and half crystal essence. Due to the high alcohol content, you shouldn't drink this straight. Instead, take 5 to 7 drops under your tongue or mixed in your water.

- If you used oil, no other preservative is needed, but it should be stored in a dark glass jar in a cool dry place so the oil doesn't go rancid.

- Don't forget to label your crystal creations!

CRYSTAL REMEDY FOR ANXIETY

Make a crystal essence using distilled or spring water and blue lace agate, lepidolite, and smoky quartz. I like to place my essence in the full moonlight for this recipe. Once the essence is made, fill a dark glass dropper bottle with half essence and half vodka. Place 5 to 7 drops under your tongue at the first sign of anxiety. Repeat every 20 minutes until anxiety subsides.

CLEANSING SPRAY AND RECHARGING SPRAY

Make crystal essence with the crystals listed below for each spray. Take a sterile dark glass bottle with a spritzer top and fill halfway with your prepared crystal essence. Fill the other half with witch hazel. Then, using a dropper, add 15 drops of each essential oil. Shake well before each use.

CLEANSING SPRAY

Black tourmaline, hematite, shungite, smoky quartz, frankincense essential oil, lavender essential oil

RECHARGING SPRAY

Carnelian, citrine, selenite, quartz, bergamot essential oil, rosemary essential oil

I use these for everything! A quick clean and charge for my crystals, for clearing before a ritual, and grounding myself when I feel disconnected.

CITRINE

ROSEMARY

SMOKEY
QUARTZ

LAVENDER

RECORD YOUR GEM ESSENCE RECIPES: ELIXIRS AND COMBOS

NAME: _____

Purpose: _____

Ingredients:

_____   _____

_____   _____

_____   _____

Notes:

_____

_____

_____

· ·

NAME: _____

Purpose: _____

Ingredients:

_____   _____

_____   _____

_____   _____

Notes:

_____

_____

_____

NAME: _____

Purpose: _____

Ingredients:

_____   _____

_____   _____

_____   _____

NOTES:

_____

_____

_____

_____

_____

NAME: _____

Purpose: _____

Ingredients:

_____   _____

_____   _____

_____   _____

Notes:

_____

_____

_____

_____

GEM ESSENCE RECIPES

NAME: _____

Purpose: _____

Ingredients:

_____   _____

_____   _____

_____   _____

Notes:

_____

_____

_____

_____

....

NAME: _____

Purpose: _____

Ingredients:

_____   _____

_____   _____

_____   _____

Notes:

_____

_____

_____

NAME: _____

Purpose: _____

Ingredients:

_____   _____

_____   _____

_____   _____

Notes:

_____

_____

_____

_____

....

NAME: _____

Purpose: _____

Ingredients:

_____   _____

_____   _____

_____   _____

Notes:

_____

_____

_____

_____

GEM ESSENCE RECIPES

NAME: _____

Purpose: _____

Ingredients:

_____   _____

_____   _____

_____   _____

Notes:

_____

_____

_____

_____

....

NAME: _____

Purpose: _____

Ingredients:

_____   _____

_____   _____

_____   _____

Notes:

_____

_____

_____

NAME: _____

Purpose: _____

Ingredients:

_____   _____

_____   _____

_____   _____

Notes:

_____

_____

_____

_____

· ·

NAME: _____

Purpose: _____

Ingredients:

_____   _____

_____   _____

_____   _____

Notes:

_____

_____

_____

_____

CRYSTAL GRIDS

Crystal grids consist of a clear intention, coordinating crystals, and sacred geometry used in combination to achieve a specific goal. When all the parts are combined, it creates a powerful tool for transformation and manifestation. Let's go over the components of a crystal grid and then explore how to make one for ourselves.

GRID COMPONENTS:

Choose your intention: Your intention is what turns on and powers your grid. It can be big or small and cover any area of life you desire. It should be something that holds a strong emotional pull.

Choose your path: The path your grid takes is the design you choose from sacred geometry. Sacred geometry makes up the patterns of our existence and we assign these patterns sacred meaning. Your grid design should harmonize with your intention and crystal selection. There are many designs from which to choose. Print one you find online, buy a cloth with design, or just draw freehand.

CIRCLE: Protection, oneness, cycles, beginning

SPIRAL: Expansion, growth, moving energy outward, awakening, a path to something

TRIANGLE: Connecting to the spirit world, balancing body, mind, and spirit, expansion

SQUARE: Balance, grounding, safety, setting boundaries

SUNBURST: Radiates or draws energy

VESICA PISCIS: Harmony, coming together, merging, union

 PENTAGRAM: Manifestation, protection, attracting abundance, nature

 HEXAGRAM: Self-improvement, cleansing

 TRIQUETRA: Letting go, breaking old patterns, friendship, trinity

CHOOSE CRYSTALS:

FOCUS STONE: For the center of the grid; draws energy into the grid and amplifies it

WAY STONES: Surrounds focus stone; helper crystals that provide energy needed to manifest goal

DESIRE STONES: Outermost stones; use the energy they gather and dispense for manifesting final goal

ACTIVATION WAND: Crystal point or wand (typically quartz) used to direct the energy flow

PERIMETER STONES (OPTIONAL): Placed around the outside of the grid, they are barriers that keep away unwanted energies and interference

CHOOSE VISUALS: Pictures, candles, symbols, or other items that you feel connect you to the grid's purpose.

LOCATION: Grids can be placed in your home or office, in the ground, or around a person using the principles of feng shui or your intuition. Just don't place it where energy will be blocked, such as a dark corner.

GRID BUILDING:

1. GATHER SUPPLIES and make sure your crystals are cleansed and charged.

2. CLEANSE AND GROUND YOURSELF and space with sacred smoke or spray. Take several deep breaths to still your mind.

3. SET YOUR GRID INTENTION. You can even write it down and place it in the center of the grid or underneath it

4. PLACE YOUR VISUALS AND GRID DESIGN.

5. ASSEMBLE THE GRID. When I place each stone, I hold it and ask it to use its energy to assist me in manifesting my intention. Place focus stone, place ways stones, place desire stones, and then place perimeter stones.

6. VISUALIZE YOUR GOAL and what it looks and feels like to have it completed. Then touch your activation wand to your forehead. Finally, touch the focus stone. Feel the grid power on and flow with energy. You could also trace the path of energy with your wand from the perimeter inward. Just do what feels right for you.

7. SAY HEARTFELT WORDS OF THANKS

8. SPEND TIME WITH YOUR GRID. Sit with it, visualize, meditate, or just say an affirmation whenever you see it.

9. DISMANTLE YOUR GRID. I like to leave mine up for an entire moon cycle, but again, use your own intuition to determine what is right for you. Clear and recharge all the stones you used.

PICTURE OR DIAGRAM OF YOUR GRID

NAME: _____ Date created: _____

Intention/purpose: _____

_____

_____

Focus Stone: _____

Way Stones: _____

Desire Stones: _____

Activation Wand: _____

Perimeter Stones: _____

Location placed: _____

Visuals used: _____

_____

Notes: _____

_____

CRYSTAL GRIDS

PICTURE OR DIAGRAM OF YOUR GRID

NAME: _____ Date created: _____

Intention/purpose: _____

_____

_____

Focus Stone: _____

Way Stones: _____

Desire Stones: _____

Activation Wand: _____

Perimeter Stones: _____

Location placed: _____

Visuals used: _____

_____

Notes: _____

_____

PICTURE OR DIAGRAM OF YOUR GRID

NAME: _____ Date created: _____

Intention/purpose: _____

_____

_____

Focus Stone: _____

Way Stones: _____

Desire Stones: _____

Activation Wand: _____

Perimeter Stones: _____

Location placed: _____

Visuals used: _____

_____

Notes: _____

_____

PICTURE OR DIAGRAM OF YOUR GRID

NAME: _____ Date created: _____

Intention/purpose: _____

_____

_____

Focus Stone: _____

Way Stones: _____

Desire Stones: _____

Activation Wand: _____

Perimeter Stones: _____

Location placed: _____

Visuals used: _____

_____

Notes: _____

_____

PICTURE OR DIAGRAM OF YOUR GRID

NAME: _____ Date created: _____

Intention/purpose: _____

_____

_____

Focus Stone: _____

Way Stones: _____

Desire Stones: _____

Activation Wand: _____

Perimeter Stones: _____

Location placed: _____

Visuals used: _____

_____

Notes: _____

_____

CRYSTAL CORRESPONDENCES

Use this section as a quick reference when you want to combine your crystal work with other elements that have the same goal or intent.

CRYSTALS AND CHAKRAS

The chakras are the energy centers of our body and can get blocked or be out of balance. When this happens, the stagnant energy begins to manifest as aliments in our physical, mental, emotional, and spiritual bodies. This chart can assist you in choosing the right stone to work with when performing chakra meditations and chakra healing, which help clear blocks and restore wholeness.

NUMBER	NAME
1st	Root
2nd	Sacral
3rd	Solar plexus
4th	Heart
5th	Throat
6th	Third eye
7th	Crown

LOCATION	SANSKRIT NAME	COLOR	FUNCTION	AFFIRMATION	CRYSTALS PAIRING
Located at the base of the spine	Muladhara	Red	Center of balance and stability; your protective force field	I am safe.	Smoky quartz, black tourmaline, garnet, red jasper
Located between genitals and naval	Svadhisthana	Orange	Creativity, sexuality, the opening for inspiration	I am creative.	Carnelian, amber, orange calcite, sunstone
Located at the navel	Manipura	Yellow	Center for personal power, confidence, and the energy to manifest our creations	I am full of power.	Citrine, tiger's eye, pyrite
Located center of chest, between breasts or pectoral muscles	Anahata	Green	Center for love and compassion and regulates energy flow	I am loved.	Aventurine, rhodochrosite, rose quartz, amazonite
Located at the throat	Vishuddha	Blue	Wisdom, communication, and speaking your truth	I am truth.	Blue lace agate, turquoise, angelite, aquamarine
Located at the forehead	Ajna	Indigo	Center for intuition; opens us to our divine nature	I am divine.	Moldavite, lapis lazuli, sodalite, amethyst
Located at the top of the head	Sahasrara	Violet	Center for connecting to your creator and opening to divine wisdom	I am infinite.	Super 7, spirit quartz, apophyllite, selenite

CRYSTALS AND THE ZODIAC

Working with the crystals that pair with your sun, moon, and rising sign can provide you with guidance from the universe on your own inner workings. It is a great way to explore your position in the zodiac and use it for personal growth and discovery.

♈ **ARIES**   ♉ **TAURUS**   ♊ **GEMINI**   ♋ **CANCER**

♌ **LEO**   ♍ **VIRGO**   ♎ **LIBRA**   ♏ **SCORPIO**

♐ **SAGITTARIUS**   ♑ **CAPRICORN**   **AQUARIUS**   **PISCES**

ZODIAC NAME	SYMBOL	SUN SIGN DATES	CRYSTAL PAIRING
ARIES	The ram	March 21 to April 19	Amethyst, citrine, fire agate, garnet, kunzite
TAURUS	The bull	April 20 to May 20	Emerald, malachite, rose quartz, sapphire, pink mangano
GEMINI	The twins	May 21 to June 20	Agate, aquamarine, citrine, serpentine, chrysocolla
CANCER	The crab	June 21 to July 22	Carnelian, calcite, opal, moonstone, chalcedony
LEO	The lion	July 23 to August 22	Tiger's eye, quartz, golden beryl, onyx, amber
VIRGO	The maiden	August 23 to September 22	Amazonite, moss agate, sugilite, peridot, sapphire
LIBRA	The scales	August 23 to October 22	Bloodstone, lapis lazuli, jade, green tourmaline, emerald
SCORPIO	The scorpion	October 23 to November 21	Malachite, obsidian, rhodochrosite, topaz, ametrine
SAGITTARIUS	The archer	November 22 to December 21	Sodalite, turquoise, labradorite, chalcedony, amethyst
CAPRICORN	The goat	December 22 to January 19	Jet, onyx, black tourmaline, smoky quartz, magnetite
AQUARIUS	The water bearer	January 20 to February 18	Celestite, moonstone, labradorite, amethyst, angelite
PISCES	The fish	February 19 to March 20	Fluorite, blue lace agate, turquoise, aquamarine, bloodstone

INTERNAL CRYSTAL STRUCTURES

All true crystals have one of seven possible repeating atomic lattices (geometric patterns) that make up the crystal's internal structure. These patterns help to identify a crystal on a physical level, but on the metaphysical level, they help us understand one of the components that makes up a crystal's unique vibrational frequency.

PICTURE	STRUCTURE NAME	DESCRIPTION	CORRESPONDING USE	CRYSTAL EXAMPLES
	Hexagonal	Resembles a 3D hexagon	New beginning, manifestation, energizes, amplifies, attracts	Apatite, aquamarine, emerald, morganite
	Isometric	Square cube structure	Focuses energy, stabilizes, grounds, personal improvement, drives passion	Garnet, fluorite, lapis lazuli, diamond
	Monoclinic	3D parallelogram	Protective, expands, facilitates spiritual growth	Lepidolite, malachite, jade, howlite, serpentine
	Orthorhombic	Inner pyramid or diamond shaped structure	Removes blocks, purifies, increases flow, cleanses	Celestite, peridot, topaz, danburite, iolite
	Tetragonal	Rectangular structure	Helper, attracts specific energies, resolves issues, magnetic	Chalcopyrite, zircon, rutilated quartz
	Triclinic	No right angle, 3 inclined axes	Defends, harmonizes energies, restores balance, repels and absorbs unwanted energy	Amazonite, labradorite, kyanite, aventurine
	Amorphous	No lattice or crystal structure	Rapid energy flow, release, catalyst for growth	Amber, moldavite, opal, pearl, obsidian, tekite

EXTERNAL CRYSTAL SHAPES

Crystal shapes can occur naturally or be cut and polished to make all kinds of cool-looking effects. Sometimes it's not just so they look pretty. The way a stone is cut or polished won't change that stone's energy frequency, but the shape can affect how the crystal's energy is directed and used. Here are some of the basic shapes.

PICTURE	SHAPE NAME	PURPOSE
	Sphere / ball	Restores and balances energy, radiates energy evenly all around
	Cluster	Unifies energy, directs the energy of a space, can diffuse negative energy and amplify positive energy
	Terminated point	Use the point to gather energy toward you or point away to draw energy off.
	Double terminated point	Aligns and balances energy. Emits and receives energy in both directions. Breaks up energy.
	Geode	Protective; conserves energy and amplifies energy in a slow, even release.

PICTURE	SHAPE NAME	PURPOSE
	Egg	Strengthens and rebalances energy.
	Cube	Grounds, connects with earth energy, transforms negative to positive.
	Heart	Amplifies healing energy and love energy.
	Pyramid	Manifests, removes blocks, and amplifies strongly.
	Wand	Channels energy in a specific direction.
	Palm stone	Aligns and attracts energy.
	Raw	The crystal in its natural state. More aligned to the energy of the Earth.
	Tumbled	Can be more easily worn close to the body (such as in a bra) for daily connection, grounding, and healing.

COLOR ENERGIES AND CRYSTALS

Like the crystal lattice structure, the color is another component that helps us determine a crystal's energetic properties.

BLACK AND GREY: Protection, banishing negativity, grounding, working with the shadow self, exploring the unknown, creating boundaries, detoxifying, stopping addiction, dealing with anxiety and fear, past life work

BROWN: Earth connection, grounding, balancing physical and emotional issues, the home, rebirth, renewal, purifying and absorbing toxins, centeredness

RED: Action, vitality, power, intensity, passion, grounding, energy, stamina, stability, safety and security, helping depression, inner strength, sensuality, stimulating, life force, fertility

ORANGE: Facilitates big changes, creativity, personal integrity, sexuality, self-identification, happiness, joy, ambition, freedom, pleasure, community

YELLOW AND GOLD: Confidence, self-worth, self-esteem, self-love, self-identity, willpower, attraction, beauty, creativity, friendships, happiness, balance of power change, adventure, success, balancing emotions and intellect, clarity, helping depression

GREEN: Growth, change, money, abundance, kindness, reduces anger, accomplishment, balance, courage, generosity, renewal, calming, emotional healing

BLUE AND INDIGO: Truth, wisdom, soothing and calming, loyalty, listening, self-expression, creative expression, speaking your truth, integrity, awareness, business, communication, emotions, consciousness, clarity

VIOLET AND PURPLE: Spirituality, divinity, intuition, intellect, reason, healing, loyalty, devotion, improving memory, critical thinking, enhancing sleep, psychic ability, astral realm, enlightenment, manifestation, concentration, inspiration, dreams

PINK: Compassion, kindness, forgiveness, unconditional love, romantic love, affection, blessings, friendship, emotions, marriage, gentleness, comfort, emotional healing, trauma acceptance, calming

WHITE AND CLEAR: Purification, new beginning, divinity, peace, connection to higher realms, cleansing, blessings, harmony, healing, divine guidance

MOON PHASES AND CRYSTALS

Moon phases and crystals go hand and hand. If you use the moon phase for manifesting in your life, then the corresponding crystals can aid in that manifestation. The phases can also assist in determining what moon phase to cleanse and charge your crystal in to achieve a specific purpose.

MOON PHASE	BENEFITS	AFFIRMATIONS	CRYSTAL
NEW MOON	New beginnings, blessing, wishes	Set new intentions or goals and let go of what no longer serves you.	Clear quartz
WAXING CRESCENT	Prepare and get clear, progress, wisdom, expansion, plan, strengthen and fortify	Get clear about your intentions or goals, so you know why you want them and what it will mean when they come to pass.	Rose quartz
FIRST QUARTER	Inspired action, bravery, communication, attract prosperity, acceleration	Let your intuition guide you to take inspired actions toward your intentions or goals.	Carnelian
WAXING GIBBOUS	Perseverance, discernment, surrender, acceptance, organization, peace	As setbacks or mistakes arise, release them and stay in the flow. Trust the process and keep going.	Citrine
FULL MOON	Celebration, completion, achievement, full of power, wholeness, release patterns, productivity	Celebrate and give thanks for your journey thus far and all that has come to pass	Labradorite
WANING GIBBOUS	Opening, receiving, letting go, boundaries, declutter, forgiveness	Open yourself and your heart to receive the unlimited abundance of the universe. Bless and be blessed.	Aquamarine
LAST QUARTER	Release the struggle, strength, new understanding, wisdom, transformation, transitions	Reflect on struggles that did not serve you, accept them as teachers, and release them.	Rhodochrosite
WANING CRESCENT	Self-love and rest, release, solitude, renewal, endings	It is time to rest, renew, and pamper yourself. Honor where you are and each step of the journey thus far.	Bloodstone

MINI CRYSTALPEDIA

These are not your typical crystal descriptions. I find many crystal descriptions very confusing. The descriptions never seem to go into detail about what the crystals protect you from or what kind of energy are they good for. I received the following descriptions through intuitively listening to crystals. I encourage you to do the same with each of your crystals, but I also offer you mine as some guidance along the way.

WHITE / COLORLESS CRYSTALS

APOPHYLLITE: *I embrace the present.*

CHAKRA: Third eye, crown

When your mind keeps running through worries from the past or fears for the future, apophyllite will help you to silence the thinking mind, and to become present and able to enjoy the moment in front of you.

CLEAR QUARTZ: *My body, mind, and spirit are balanced.*

CHAKRA: All

Clear quartz may be very common, but it is also one of the most powerful crystals. I could write a whole book on the amazing capabilities of this crystal. It is pretty much the Swiss army knife of crystals. This stone can balance energy, amplify it, focus it, purify it, and conduct it. Perfect to use with any other crystal to amplify its energy.

HERKIMER DIAMOND: *I am aligned with my soul's purpose.*

CHAKRA: Third eye, crown

Herkimer is there when you need to connect back to your free spirit that has been lost in the bustle of everyday life. It lets the real you shine through anything that may be blocking your brilliance.

MOONSTONE: *I flow effortlessly with the rhythms of the Earth.*

CHAKRA: Sacral, third eye

When you are ready for deep emotional work and strengthening your intuition, moonstone will assist. It has a beautiful ability to help keep you in the flow and accept the natural rhythms of life, whether they are up or down.

SELENITE: *I allow peace and purity to fill me.*

CHAKRA: Crown

Your multipurpose cleaner! It will clean your aura and the built-up gunk energy in your home. Blockages be gone! Don't be afraid to wave it around everywhere. The great part of cleaning things up is the clarity and peace that comes after.

SPIRIT QUARTZ: *I honor all life. I am in harmony with all life.*

CHAKRA: Crown

Use this crystal to go beyond your limited self-view and feel a oneness with all of life. Let it open you to universal love. It elevates good vibes and creates harmony.

AMPHIBOLE QUARTZ: *I open myself to healing that transcends all time and space.*

CHAKRA: Sacral, crown, third eye

The high vibrations of this crystal expand our consciousness and connect us to the unseen, where we experience some serious spiritual growth. Work with it to heal trauma that may have traveled with you through many lives.

CARNELIAN: *I am aligned with the flow of passion and creativity.*

CHAKRA: Root, sacral

Are you feeling bored, lifeless, and without creativity? Carnelian infuses you, and situations, with energy and vitality. When you lack drive, this beauty is the perfect pick-me-up full of passion and let's-do-this attitude.

GARNET: *I have the courage to keep moving forward.*

CHAKRA: Root

Garnet will take a scattered mind and life and bring it much-needed focused energy. Keep it close when you need courage to do something new or face something you have been avoiding.

ORANGE CALCITE: *I feel energized and alive in my body, mind, and spirit.*

CHAKRA: Sacral

Orange calcite is a shot of happy energy, so use it when you are feeling down and under the weather. When suffering from depression, this stone can be uplifting to your body, mind, and spirit.

RED JASPER: *I have the determination and drive to reach my goals.*

CHAKRA: Sacral, root

Red jasper will feed your willpower until you achieve your desires. This stone doesn't understand what it is to give up or quit. If you have negative mojo, red jasper will absorb it and give you some needed stress relief.

SUNSTONE: *I see only unlimited possibilities before me.*

CHAKRA: Sacral, solar plexus

Like its name, this crystal has a sunny disposition that infuses your dreams with energy. So think big and let sunstone's inspiring vibes open the door to new opportunities. This crystal is a confidence builder, so let the self-doubt fade to black and embrace the expansion it brings.

YELLOW / GOLD CRYSTALS

ASTROPHYLLITE: *I connect to the divine within me.*

CHAKRA: Crown, all

This crystal goes deep and takes us beyond our limited physical reality. It opens us so we may access our own divine guidance, allowing us to manifest our deeper purpose into physical reality. It is the light that can guide you through the darkness when you forget what all this is for.

BUMBLE BEE JASPER: *I trust my intuition to guide me.*

CHAKRA: Sacral, solar plexus

If you are questioning how to handle situations or what your next steps should be, let bumble bee jasper connect you back to your gut feelings. It will strengthen your intuition so you can hear the answers without the thinking mind butting in.

CITRINE: *I move from a place of joy and success.*

CHAKRA: Solar plexus

Citrine ain't having none of those bad vibes. It clears negative energy and bathes everything in rays of sunshine and joy. Its energy centers your being and boosts your confidence so you can manifest your way to success in all your endeavors.

MOOKAITE JASPER: *I have the clarity and wisdom to navigate any situation.*

CHAKRA: Sacral, solar plexus, third eye

Mookaite has a beautiful protective and grounding energy that anchors us to the earth so we may be nurtured and restored. It encourages us to be versatile and open so we may perceive with great clarity the situation before us. This crystal really lets your natural beauty shine.

TIGER'S EYE: *I am full of power.*

CHAKRA: Sacral, solar plexus

Tiger's eye brings out the warrior energy, igniting your inner power and courage. It is a protective stone that heightens your ability to take in a situation clearly and not be ruled by emotions. Use its powerful energy to explore new things, for it will protect you on your journey.

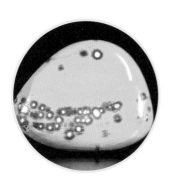

YELLOW JASPER: *I am supported and loved.*

CHAKRA: Solar plexus

Yellow jasper is like your little buddy that wants to be your friend and follow you everywhere. It will be there to catch you if you trip, offer encouragement when you start something new, give you a hug when you're sad, and protect and shield you on your Earth journey. You will find no better faithful friend.

GREEN / BLUE-GREEN CRYSTALS

AVENTURINE: *The world is abundant for all to enjoy.*

CHAKRA: Heart

When you come to a crossroads and have to make difficult choices, or it's time for a big change, aventurine is your stone to promote a positive outcome, because this crystal is one of luck and abundance. You can stay optimistic when aventurine is on your side.

AMAZONITE: *I am grateful for this beautiful life.*

CHAKRA: Heart, throat

This crystal of hope and joy is a wonderful help in making life transitions more peaceful. It opens our eyes to see the upside and be grateful for all things in our lives, instead of focusing on the negative.

MOLDAVITE: *I surrender and trust the universe to guide me.*

CHAKRA: All

Get ready, because moldavite comes crashing into your life to shake things up and push you past your boundaries. We all need a push sometimes, and this intense crystal impels you to a spiritual evolution while kindly requesting that you trust the process. If you can go with the flow and surrender, the possibilities are unlimited.

PREHNITE: *The universe assists me on my spiritual quest.*

CHAKRA: Heart, third eye

A gentle, loving stone that helps us connect to our faith in the divine and unseen magic of this world. A wonderful aid to have by your side when doing rituals, Reiki healing, tarot reading, astral projection, or any kind of metaphysical work.

SERPENTINE: *I awaken to the divine flow.*

CHAKRA: Root, crown

Serpentine assists us in shedding the past that we have been dragging around with us for too long. Through release, serpentine opens the pathway for kundalini energy to flow, offering us spiritual awakening and personal transformation.

TREE AGATE: *I am supported by the universe.*

CHAKRA: Heart

Tree agate is like a cozy blanket that makes us feel loved, safe, and secure. While relaxing in its calming embrace, hearts open and minds release negative thought patterns that have been harbored unconsciously. After working with tree agate, we are left feeling grounded and balanced.

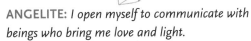

BLUE CRYSTALS

ANGELITE: *I open myself to communicate with beings who bring me love and light.*

CHAKRA: Throat, third eye

When you are looking to communicate with the angelic realm, spirit guides, or animals, this is your go-to crystal. Through working with this crystal and guides, we receive support and wisdom to enhance our earthly reality.

BLUE LACE AGATE: *Fear cannot survive in the face of truth.*

CHAKRA: Throat, third eye

Blue lace agate is the equivalent to a chill pill for those who experience anxiety and panic attacks. Living with anxiety is often the result of a traumatic experience, and this stone can help you release that trauma by encouraging you to share your truth.

CELESTITE: *I have the clarity to receive divine guidance and the wisdom to use it for my highest good.*

CHAKRA: Third eye, crown

When you seek divine guidance from a sign, through prayer, or in a tarot reading, celestite will help bring clarity to the answers you receive, and wisdom to use them for your highest good.

KYANITE: *My body and spirit are aligned and I am whole.*

CHAKRA: Throat, all

Grab some kyanite when you need a quick tune-up. This crystal will get your energy flowing freely and align your chakras, bringing wholeness to the body and spirit. It has the power to cut through blocks and negative energy.

LAPIS LAZULI: *I speak my truth from my spirit with confidence.*

CHAKRA: Third eye, throat

This crystal will help you express your spiritual power and speak your truth with confidence as insults and attacks are repelled and rendered powerless. Lapis aids you in standing up for what you believe in and letting go of unhealthy emotional ties.

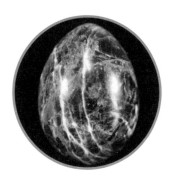

SODALITE: *I see through illusions with my intuitive knowing.*

CHAKRA: Throat

Whether you are a passionate truth seeker or just someone who needs clarity and answers to a convoluted situation, sodalite can assist. It will dissolve confusion, illusions, and destructive mental conditioning so you may discover solutions with a heightened intuitive knowing.

PURPLE CRYSTALS

AMETHYST: *I am a spiritual baddass!*

CHAKRA: Third eye, crown

In the journey of self-discovery, you will undoubtedly encounter major transitions that transform you and life as you knew it before. Amethyst is the perfect companion for this journey. It will hold your hand and offer you purifying and cleansing energy. It encourages you to keep going and leads you closer to fulfillment.

FLUORITE: *My life flows in effortless balance.*

CHAKRA: Third eye

Fluorite has this adulting thing down, so if you don't, then this stone is for you. It helps bring organization, stability, and focus to your life while sending negativity and chaos packing. When the mess is all cleaned up, you can relax in the harmony it has imparted to your life.

CHAROITE: *When I serve another, I serve myself.*

CHAKRA: Heart, crown

Charoite assists you when you do the soul's work of serving others and helping humanity. It can provide clear insight for understanding the heart of a situation and attuning to the needs of others.

LEPIDOLITE: *I am not my thoughts.*

CHAKRA: Third eye

Lepidolite provides a calming presence when your mind is consumed by obsessive thoughts and irrational fears. It will ease phobias and nervous compulsions by helping you see the origin of the suffering. Let lepidolite be the thing you grab to relax and find peace in your mind.

LITHIUM QUARTZ: *I am not my emotions.*

CHAKRA: Third eye, all

Whether your mind is going warp speed in a hundred directions, or has checked out mentally to a state of numbness, lithium quartz may assist you in achieving balance.

SUGILITE: *I am aligned with my soul's purpose.*

CHAKRA: Third eye, crown, heart

Do not despair, sugilite is here! If you are feeling lost in life right now, it will help you get back on track and realign with your soul's purpose, or be your shield should you have the courage to go deeper on a spiritual quest.

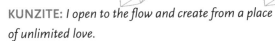

PINK CRYSTALS

KUNZITE: *I open to the flow and create from a place of unlimited love.*

CHAKRA: Heart

Kunzite helps us remove mental roadblocks that keep us in old patterns and blind us to our boundless potential. It assists in embodying our true unlimited nature to receive inspired ideas and creativity that comes from the heart.

MANGANO CALCITE: *I open my heart to give and receive unconditional love.*

CHAKRA: Heart

If you are a total Grinch, get yourself some mangano calcite. This crystal is all about opening the heart to unconditional love. You will turn that Grinch attitude into a gentle sense of peace and calm. You will find yourself feeling more generous and forgiving as well.

MORGANITE: *I deepen my love by connecting and sharing it with others.*

CHAKRA: Heart

Morganite opens our hearts to attract and receive love from another person. It facilitates the building of a love connection that is based on soul communion with another.

RHODOCHROSITE: *I am ready to release my pain and make space for joy.*

CHAKRA: Heart, solar plexus

Sometimes the pain in your heart is so deep you don't know how to even begin to process it. Rhodochrosite lends us a sympathetic eye to look at these feelings with compassion, and let them move through and out of us. It will ease the pain but also let you know that you are not alone.

RHODONITE: *I open my heart to the healing power of forgiveness.*

CHAKRA: Heart

When your heart is heavy with regret or resentment and you can't seem to forgive and forget, call on rhodonite. It will help you process these feelings, cultivate compassion and forgiveness, and forget the past pain.

ROSE QUARTZ: *I accept all and know it is part of the divine plan.*

CHAKRA: Heart

Soothe the fearful stressed mind with rose quartz. It helps us silence the mind, and see the beauty and perfection in all that is in the world, and in you. We descend into peace because we trust the process of the universe, knowing all is as it should be.

ARAGONITE: *Through grounding, I am nourished and my energy is replenished.*

CHAKRA: Root

Is your head always in the clouds? Do you love to daydream, and do you have a rich imaginative playground that captivates your attention? Well, aragonite brings you back down to Earth. Its beautiful, supportive nature can help recharge you, so you can get back to that imagination of yours.

NUUMMITE: *The magic is in me.*

CHAKRA: Root, all

We all have unique talents and gifts that may be obscured or underdeveloped. Nuummite invites you to tap into your hidden magic. Let it guide you on the journey to discover your unseen powers and magical talents, so you may use them for your highest good.

OBSIDIAN: *Through letting go of the past, I am free.*

CHAKRA: Root

Does your mind accumulate boxes of worries, fears, regrets, anger, and so on? It's just a bunch of junk you don't want, but like a hoarder, you can't seem to throw it away. Soon there is no space left inside. What can you do? Obsidian will come with its big junk removal truck and help clean the place out with fierce determination. You will have no choice but to face things. But the satisfaction of a clean, shiny space afterward is so worth it.

SHUNGITE: *I recycle low energy and purify it for healing.*

CHAKRA: All

This ancient healing stone is your shield against toxins and pollutants in your environment. It can be a great immune boost or detox for your body, mind, and spirit. When you think of shungite, think shield, absorb, purify, and protect. This stone has your back.

SMOKY QUARTZ: *I go forward with courage, knowing all has a purpose in my soul's growth.*

CHAKRA: Root

Smoky quartz is like a light that guides us through dark times. Things will still be hard, but it helps us to tolerate them, balance our emotions, and keep going forward. Once we get through the difficult times, it will help us gain a spiritual understanding of the purpose of our trials.

TOURMALINE: *I interact with others while anchored in my seat of balance and harmony.*

CHAKRA: Root, all

Tourmaline is a crystal you want to bring just about everywhere. It helps us to see the bright side of all situations. Its gift is balancing energy, so no matter where you are working, traveling, shopping at the market, or doing anything else, tourmaline steps in to neutralize low energy and restore harmony.

PART 2

THE
JOURNAL

THIS SECTION IS TRULY THE HEART OF THIS BOOK, AND WAS THE MAIN INSPIRATION FOR WRITING IT. I wanted a place to create my own personal crystal logbook. A place to record the names of crystals, so I would never again forget one. A place to put my crystals' unique stories, where they came from, and their special traits. A place to record my own intuitive feeling about a crystal's properties. A place to keep pictures of my crystals and all the stuff I do with them. It is my hope that this section will become your personal reference guide and your keepsake album of your unique crystal collection.

USING THE JOURNAL

Here's an example of the Crystal Journal Pages that follow.

Name: _Crystal name_

Date of acquisition: _____

Date you purchased or received

Place: _____

Where acquired, or who gave it

to you

*INSERT PICTURE OR
DRAWING OF YOUR CRYSTAL.*

Water friendly   **Sunlight friendly**

Hardness: _____ **Chakra:** _____

Crystalline structure: _____

Country of origin: _____

MENTAL/EMOTIONAL PROPERTIES	PHYSICAL PROPERTIES	SPIRITUAL PROPERTIES
Use this section to	You can fill it in using	other books or websites
create a quick reference	your own intuition or	to help you
for your crystal	check out	

Intuitive vibe

This section is to record how the crystal feels to you on all levels of your being.

Do you feel calm? Does it feel hot? And so on. There is no wrong
way to do this part; just trust your inner voice.

Uses

This is for recording ways you may utilize the stone to enhance your life.

Example: Place tourmaline in all four corners of home for protection.

Notes

Use this section to record whatever you want.

I enjoy using this section to record my crystal's story of ways I
have used it.
Example: · Meditated with it for 30 days. · Used in studio for
creativity. · Used in healing crystal grid.

Affirmation

Writing an affirmation or mantra for your crystal can help build your relationship with it.

Each time you hold the stone and use it, you create an anchor in
your own mind, but also exchange energy with your crystal.

Name: _____

Date of acquisition: _____

_____

Place: _____

_____

_____

*INSERT PICTURE OR
DRAWING OF YOUR CRYSTAL.*

Water friendly   Sunlight friendly

Hardness: _____ Chakra: _____

Crystalline structure: _____

Country of origin: _____

MENTAL/EMOTIONAL PROPERTIES	PHYSICAL PROPERTIES	SPIRITUAL PROPERTIES

Intuitive vibe

_____

_____

_____

_____

Uses

_____

_____

_____

_____

_____

Notes

_____

_____

_____

_____

_____

Affirmation

_____

_____

_____

_____

Name: _____

Date of acquisition: _____

_____

Place: _____

_____

_____

*INSERT PICTURE OR
DRAWING OF YOUR CRYSTAL.*

Water friendly   Sunlight friendly

Hardness: _____ Chakra: _____

Crystalline structure: _____

Country of origin: _____

MENTAL/EMOTIONAL PROPERTIES	PHYSICAL PROPERTIES	SPIRITUAL PROPERTIES

Intuitive vibe

_____

_____

_____

_____

Uses

_____

_____

_____

_____

_____

Notes

_____

_____

_____

_____

_____

Affirmation

_____

_____

_____

_____

Name: _____

Date of acquisition: _____

_____

Place: _____

_____

_____

*INSERT PICTURE OR
DRAWING OF YOUR CRYSTAL.*

Water friendly   Sunlight friendly

Hardness: _____ Chakra: _____

Crystalline structure: _____

Country of origin: _____

MENTAL/EMOTIONAL PROPERTIES	PHYSICAL PROPERTIES	SPIRITUAL PROPERTIES

Intuitive vibe

_____

_____

_____

_____

Uses

_____

_____

_____

_____

_____

Notes

_____

_____

_____

_____

Affirmation

_____

_____

_____

_____

Name: _____

Date of acquisition: _____

_____

Place: _____

_____

_____

INSERT PICTURE OR DRAWING OF YOUR CRYSTAL.

Water friendly   Sunlight friendly

Hardness: _____ Chakra: _____

Crystalline structure: _____

Country of origin: _____

MENTAL/EMOTIONAL PROPERTIES	PHYSICAL PROPERTIES	SPIRITUAL PROPERTIES

Intuitive vibe

_____

_____

_____

_____

Uses

_____

_____

_____

_____

_____

Notes

_____

_____

_____

_____

_____

Affirmation

_____

_____

_____

_____

Name: _____

Date of acquisition: _____

_____

Place: _____

_____

_____

*INSERT PICTURE OR
DRAWING OF YOUR CRYSTAL.*

Water friendly   Sunlight friendly

Hardness: _____ Chakra: _____

Crystalline structure: _____

Country of origin: _____

MENTAL/EMOTIONAL PROPERTIES	PHYSICAL PROPERTIES	SPIRITUAL PROPERTIES

Intuitive vibe

_____

_____

_____

_____

Uses

_____

_____

_____

_____

_____

Notes

_____

_____

_____

_____

_____

Affirmation

_____

_____

_____

_____

Name: _____

Date of acquisition: _____

_____

Place: _____

_____

_____

*INSERT PICTURE OR
DRAWING OF YOUR CRYSTAL.*

Water friendly   Sunlight friendly

Hardness: _____ Chakra: _____

Crystalline structure: _____

Country of origin: _____

MENTAL/EMOTIONAL PROPERTIES	PHYSICAL PROPERTIES	SPIRITUAL PROPERTIES

Intuitive vibe

_____

_____

_____

_____

Uses

_____

_____

_____

_____

Notes

_____

_____

_____

_____

_____

Affirmation

_____

_____

_____

_____

Name: _____

Date of acquisition: _____

_____

Place: _____

_____

_____

*INSERT PICTURE OR
DRAWING OF YOUR CRYSTAL.*

Water friendly   Sunlight friendly

Hardness: _____ Chakra: _____

Crystalline structure: _____

Country of origin: _____

MENTAL/EMOTIONAL PROPERTIES	PHYSICAL PROPERTIES	SPIRITUAL PROPERTIES

Intuitive vibe

_____

_____

_____

_____

Uses

_____

_____

_____

_____

_____

Notes

_____

_____

_____

_____

Affirmation

_____

_____

_____

_____

Name: _____

Date of acquisition: _____

_____

Place: _____

_____

_____

INSERT PICTURE OR DRAWING OF YOUR CRYSTAL.

Water friendly   Sunlight friendly

Hardness: _____ Chakra: _____

Crystalline structure: _____

Country of origin: _____

MENTAL/EMOTIONAL PROPERTIES	PHYSICAL PROPERTIES	SPIRITUAL PROPERTIES

Intuitive vibe

_____

_____

_____

_____

Uses

_____

_____

_____

_____

_____

Notes

_____

_____

_____

_____

_____

Affirmation

_____

_____

_____

_____

Name: _____

Date of acquisition: _____

_____

Place: _____

_____

*INSERT PICTURE OR
DRAWING OF YOUR CRYSTAL.*

Water friendly   Sunlight friendly

Hardness: _____ Chakra: _____

Crystalline structure: _____

Country of origin: _____

MENTAL/EMOTIONAL PROPERTIES	PHYSICAL PROPERTIES	SPIRITUAL PROPERTIES

Intuitive vibe

_____

_____

_____

_____

Uses

_____

_____

_____

_____

_____

Notes

_____

_____

_____

_____

_____

Affirmation

_____

_____

_____

_____

Name: _____

Date of acquisition: _____

_____

Place: _____

_____

_____

INSERT PICTURE OR
DRAWING OF YOUR CRYSTAL.

Water friendly   Sunlight friendly

Hardness: _____ Chakra: _____

Crystalline structure: _____

Country of origin: _____

MENTAL/EMOTIONAL PROPERTIES	PHYSICAL PROPERTIES	SPIRITUAL PROPERTIES

Intuitive vibe

_____

_____

_____

_____

Uses

_____

_____

_____

_____

_____

Notes

_____

_____

_____

_____

_____

Affirmation

_____

_____

_____

_____

Name: _____

Date of acquisition: _____

_____

Place: _____

_____

_____

INSERT PICTURE OR
DRAWING OF YOUR CRYSTAL.

Water friendly   Sunlight friendly

Hardness: _____ Chakra: _____

Crystalline structure: _____

Country of origin: _____

MENTAL/EMOTIONAL PROPERTIES	PHYSICAL PROPERTIES	SPIRITUAL PROPERTIES

Intuitive vibe

_____

_____

_____

_____

Uses

_____

_____

_____

_____

_____

Notes

_____

_____

_____

_____

_____

Affirmation

_____

_____

_____

_____

Name: _____

Date of acquisition: _____

_____

Place: _____

_____

_____

*INSERT PICTURE OR
DRAWING OF YOUR CRYSTAL.*

Water friendly   Sunlight friendly

Hardness: _____ Chakra: _____

Crystalline structure: _____

Country of origin: _____

MENTAL/EMOTIONAL PROPERTIES	PHYSICAL PROPERTIES	SPIRITUAL PROPERTIES

Intuitive vibe

_____

_____

_____

_____

Uses

_____

_____

_____

_____

_____

Notes

_____

_____

_____

_____

_____

Affirmation

_____

_____

_____

_____

Name: _____

Date of acquisition: _____

_____

Place: _____

_____

*INSERT PICTURE OR
DRAWING OF YOUR CRYSTAL.*

_____

Water friendly   Sunlight friendly

Hardness: _____ Chakra: _____

Crystalline structure: _____

Country of origin: _____

MENTAL/EMOTIONAL PROPERTIES	PHYSICAL PROPERTIES	SPIRITUAL PROPERTIES

Intuitive vibe

_____

_____

_____

_____

Uses

_____

_____

_____

_____

_____

Notes

_____

_____

_____

_____

_____

Affirmation

_____

_____

_____

_____

Name: _____

Date of acquisition: _____

_____

Place: _____

_____

_____

INSERT PICTURE OR DRAWING OF YOUR CRYSTAL.

Water friendly   Sunlight friendly

Hardness: _____ Chakra: _____

Crystalline structure: _____

Country of origin: _____

MENTAL/EMOTIONAL PROPERTIES	PHYSICAL PROPERTIES	SPIRITUAL PROPERTIES

Intuitive vibe

_____

_____

_____

_____

Uses

_____

_____

_____

_____

_____

Notes

_____

_____

_____

_____

_____

Affirmation

_____

_____

_____

_____

Name: _____

Date of acquisition: _____

_____

Place: _____

_____

*INSERT PICTURE OR
DRAWING OF YOUR CRYSTAL.*

Water friendly   Sunlight friendly

Hardness: _____ Chakra: _____

Crystalline structure: _____

Country of origin: _____

MENTAL/EMOTIONAL PROPERTIES	PHYSICAL PROPERTIES	SPIRITUAL PROPERTIES

Intuitive vibe

_____

_____

_____

_____

Uses

_____

_____

_____

_____

_____

Notes

_____

_____

_____

_____

_____

Affirmation

_____

_____

_____

_____

Name: _____

Date of acquisition: _____

_____

Place: _____

_____

_____

*INSERT PICTURE OR
DRAWING OF YOUR CRYSTAL.*

Water friendly   Sunlight friendly

Hardness: _____ Chakra: _____

Crystalline structure: _____

Country of origin: _____

MENTAL/EMOTIONAL PROPERTIES	PHYSICAL PROPERTIES	SPIRITUAL PROPERTIES

Intuitive vibe

_____

_____

_____

_____

Uses

_____

_____

_____

_____

_____

Notes

_____

_____

_____

_____

_____

Affirmation

_____

_____

_____

_____

Name: _____

Date of acquisition: _____

_____

Place: _____

_____

INSERT PICTURE OR DRAWING OF YOUR CRYSTAL.

Water friendly   Sunlight friendly

Hardness: _____ Chakra: _____

Crystalline structure: _____

Country of origin: _____

MENTAL/EMOTIONAL PROPERTIES	PHYSICAL PROPERTIES	SPIRITUAL PROPERTIES

Intuitive vibe

_____

_____

_____

_____

Uses

_____

_____

_____

_____

_____

Notes

_____

_____

_____

_____

_____

Affirmation

_____

_____

_____

_____

Name: _____

Date of acquisition: _____

_____

Place: _____

_____

_____

INSERT PICTURE OR DRAWING OF YOUR CRYSTAL.

Water friendly   Sunlight friendly

Hardness: _____ Chakra: _____

Crystalline structure: _____

Country of origin: _____

MENTAL/EMOTIONAL PROPERTIES	PHYSICAL PROPERTIES	SPIRITUAL PROPERTIES

Intuitive vibe

_____

_____

_____

_____

Uses

_____

_____

_____

_____

_____

Notes

_____

_____

_____

_____

_____

Affirmation

_____

_____

_____

_____

Name: _____

Date of acquisition: _____

_____

Place: _____

_____

_____

INSERT PICTURE OR DRAWING OF YOUR CRYSTAL.

Water friendly   Sunlight friendly

Hardness: _____ Chakra: _____

Crystalline structure: _____

Country of origin: _____

MENTAL/EMOTIONAL PROPERTIES	PHYSICAL PROPERTIES	SPIRITUAL PROPERTIES

Intuitive vibe

_____

_____

_____

_____

Uses

_____

_____

_____

_____

Notes

_____

_____

_____

_____

_____

Affirmation

_____

_____

_____

_____

Name: _____

Date of acquisition: _____

_____

Place: _____

_____

INSERT PICTURE OR DRAWING OF YOUR CRYSTAL.

_____

Water friendly   Sunlight friendly

Hardness: _____ Chakra: _____

Crystalline structure: _____

Country of origin: _____

MENTAL/EMOTIONAL PROPERTIES	PHYSICAL PROPERTIES	SPIRITUAL PROPERTIES

Intuitive vibe

_____

_____

_____

_____

Uses

_____

_____

_____

_____

_____

Notes

_____

_____

_____

_____

_____

Affirmation

_____

_____

_____

_____

Name: _____

Date of acquisition: _____

_____

Place: _____

_____

_____

*INSERT PICTURE OR
DRAWING OF YOUR CRYSTAL.*

Water friendly   Sunlight friendly

Hardness: _____ Chakra: _____

Crystalline structure: _____

Country of origin: _____

MENTAL/EMOTIONAL PROPERTIES	PHYSICAL PROPERTIES	SPIRITUAL PROPERTIES

Intuitive vibe

_____

_____

_____

_____

Uses

_____

_____

_____

_____

_____

Notes

_____

_____

_____

_____

_____

Affirmation

_____

_____

_____

_____

Name: _____

Date of acquisition: _____

_____

Place: _____

_____

_____

*INSERT PICTURE OR
DRAWING OF YOUR CRYSTAL.*

Water friendly   Sunlight friendly

Hardness: _____ Chakra: _____

Crystalline structure: _____

Country of origin: _____

MENTAL/EMOTIONAL PROPERTIES	PHYSICAL PROPERTIES	SPIRITUAL PROPERTIES

Intuitive vibe

_____

_____

_____

_____

Uses

_____

_____

_____

_____

_____

Notes

_____

_____

_____

_____

_____

Affirmation

_____

_____

_____

_____

Name: _____

Date of acquisition: _____

_____

Place: _____

_____

_____

*INSERT PICTURE OR
DRAWING OF YOUR CRYSTAL.*

Water friendly   Sunlight friendly

Hardness: _____ Chakra: _____

Crystalline structure: _____

Country of origin: _____

MENTAL/EMOTIONAL PROPERTIES	PHYSICAL PROPERTIES	SPIRITUAL PROPERTIES

Intuitive vibe

_____

_____

_____

_____

Uses

_____

_____

_____

_____

_____

Notes

_____

_____

_____

_____

Affirmation

_____

_____

_____

_____

Name: _____

Date of acquisition: _____

_____

Place: _____

_____

INSERT PICTURE OR DRAWING OF YOUR CRYSTAL.

_____

Water friendly   Sunlight friendly

Hardness: _____ Chakra: _____

Crystalline structure: _____

Country of origin: _____

MENTAL/EMOTIONAL PROPERTIES	PHYSICAL PROPERTIES	SPIRITUAL PROPERTIES

Intuitive vibe

_____

_____

_____

_____

Uses

_____

_____

_____

_____

_____

Notes

_____

_____

_____

_____

Affirmation

_____

_____

_____

_____

Name: _____

Date of acquisition: _____

_____

Place: _____

_____

*INSERT PICTURE OR
DRAWING OF YOUR CRYSTAL.*

_____

Water friendly   Sunlight friendly

Hardness: _____ Chakra: _____

Crystalline structure: _____

Country of origin: _____

MENTAL/EMOTIONAL PROPERTIES	PHYSICAL PROPERTIES	SPIRITUAL PROPERTIES

Intuitive vibe

_____

_____

_____

_____

Uses

_____

_____

_____

_____

_____

Notes

_____

_____

_____

_____

_____

Affirmation

_____

_____

_____

_____

Name: _____

Date of acquisition: _____

_____

Place: _____

_____

*INSERT PICTURE OR
DRAWING OF YOUR CRYSTAL.*

Water friendly   Sunlight friendly

Hardness: _____ Chakra: _____

Crystalline structure: _____

Country of origin: _____

MENTAL/EMOTIONAL PROPERTIES	PHYSICAL PROPERTIES	SPIRITUAL PROPERTIES

Intuitive vibe

_____

_____

_____

_____

Uses

_____

_____

_____

_____

_____

Notes

_____

_____

_____

_____

_____

Affirmation

_____

_____

_____

_____

Name: _____

Date of acquisition: _____

_____

Place: _____

_____

_____

*INSERT PICTURE OR
DRAWING OF YOUR CRYSTAL.*

Water friendly   Sunlight friendly

Hardness: _____ Chakra: _____

Crystalline structure: _____

Country of origin: _____

MENTAL/EMOTIONAL PROPERTIES	PHYSICAL PROPERTIES	SPIRITUAL PROPERTIES

Intuitive vibe

_____

_____

_____

_____

Uses

_____

_____

_____

_____

_____

Notes

_____

_____

_____

_____

_____

Affirmation

_____

_____

_____

_____

Name: _____

Date of acquisition: _____

_____

Place: _____

_____

INSERT PICTURE OR
DRAWING OF YOUR CRYSTAL.

_____

Water friendly   Sunlight friendly

Hardness: _____ Chakra: _____

Crystalline structure: _____

Country of origin: _____

MENTAL/EMOTIONAL PROPERTIES	PHYSICAL PROPERTIES	SPIRITUAL PROPERTIES

Intuitive vibe

_____

_____

_____

_____

Uses

_____

_____

_____

_____

_____

Notes

_____

_____

_____

_____

_____

Affirmation

_____

_____

_____

_____

Name: _____

Date of acquisition: _____

_____

Place: _____

_____

*INSERT PICTURE OR
DRAWING OF YOUR CRYSTAL.*

_____

Water friendly   Sunlight friendly

Hardness: _____ Chakra: _____

Crystalline structure: _____

Country of origin: _____

MENTAL/EMOTIONAL PROPERTIES	PHYSICAL PROPERTIES	SPIRITUAL PROPERTIES

Intuitive vibe

_____

_____

_____

_____

Uses

_____

_____

_____

_____

_____

Notes

_____

_____

_____

_____

_____

Affirmation

_____

_____

_____

_____

Name: _____

Date of acquisition: _____

_____

Place: _____

_____

_____

INSERT PICTURE OR DRAWING OF YOUR CRYSTAL.

Water friendly   Sunlight friendly

Hardness: _____ Chakra: _____

Crystalline structure: _____

Country of origin: _____

MENTAL/EMOTIONAL PROPERTIES	PHYSICAL PROPERTIES	SPIRITUAL PROPERTIES

Intuitive vibe

_____

_____

_____

_____

Uses

_____

_____

_____

_____

_____

Notes

_____

_____

_____

_____

_____

Affirmation

_____

_____

_____

_____

Name: _____

Date of acquisition: _____

_____

Place: _____

_____

_____

INSERT PICTURE OR DRAWING OF YOUR CRYSTAL.

Water friendly   Sunlight friendly

Hardness: _____ Chakra: _____

Crystalline structure: _____

Country of origin: _____

MENTAL/EMOTIONAL PROPERTIES	PHYSICAL PROPERTIES	SPIRITUAL PROPERTIES

Intuitive vibe

_____

_____

_____

_____

Uses

_____

_____

_____

_____

_____

Notes

_____

_____

_____

_____

Affirmation

_____

_____

_____

_____

Name: _____

Date of acquisition: _____

_____

Place: _____

_____

_____

*INSERT PICTURE OR
DRAWING OF YOUR CRYSTAL.*

Water friendly   Sunlight friendly

Hardness: _____ Chakra: _____

Crystalline structure: _____

Country of origin: _____

MENTAL/EMOTIONAL PROPERTIES	PHYSICAL PROPERTIES	SPIRITUAL PROPERTIES

Intuitive vibe

_____

_____

_____

_____

Uses

_____

_____

_____

_____

Notes

_____

_____

_____

_____

Affirmation

_____

_____

_____

_____

Name: _____

Date of acquisition: _____

_____

Place: _____

_____

_____

*INSERT PICTURE OR
DRAWING OF YOUR CRYSTAL.*

Water friendly   Sunlight friendly

Hardness: _____ Chakra: _____

Crystalline structure: _____

Country of origin: _____

MENTAL/EMOTIONAL PROPERTIES	PHYSICAL PROPERTIES	SPIRITUAL PROPERTIES

Intuitive vibe

_____

_____

_____

_____

Uses

_____

_____

_____

_____

_____

Notes

_____

_____

_____

_____

_____

Affirmation

_____

_____

_____

_____

Name: _____

Date of acquisition: _____

_____

Place: _____

_____

_____

*INSERT PICTURE OR
DRAWING OF YOUR CRYSTAL.*

Water friendly   Sunlight friendly

Hardness: _____ Chakra: _____

Crystalline structure: _____

Country of origin: _____

MENTAL/EMOTIONAL PROPERTIES	PHYSICAL PROPERTIES	SPIRITUAL PROPERTIES

Intuitive vibe

_____

_____

_____

_____

Uses

_____

_____

_____

_____

_____

Notes

_____

_____

_____

_____

_____

Affirmation

_____

_____

_____

_____

Name: _____

Date of acquisition: _____
_____

Place: _____
_____
_____

*INSERT PICTURE OR
DRAWING OF YOUR CRYSTAL.*

Water friendly   Sunlight friendly

Hardness: _____ Chakra: _____

Crystalline structure: _____

Country of origin: _____

MENTAL/EMOTIONAL PROPERTIES	PHYSICAL PROPERTIES	SPIRITUAL PROPERTIES

Intuitive vibe

_____

_____

_____

_____

Uses

_____

_____

_____

_____

_____

Notes

_____

_____

_____

_____

_____

Affirmation

_____

_____

_____

_____

Name: _____

Date of acquisition: _____

_____

Place: _____

_____

_____

*INSERT PICTURE OR
DRAWING OF YOUR CRYSTAL.*

Water friendly   Sunlight friendly

Hardness: _____ Chakra: _____

Crystalline structure: _____

Country of origin: _____

MENTAL/EMOTIONAL PROPERTIES	PHYSICAL PROPERTIES	SPIRITUAL PROPERTIES

Intuitive vibe

_____

_____

_____

_____

Uses

_____

_____

_____

_____

_____

Notes

_____

_____

_____

_____

_____

Affirmation

_____

_____

_____

_____

Name: _____

Date of acquisition: _____

_____

Place: _____

_____

INSERT PICTURE OR DRAWING OF YOUR CRYSTAL.

Water friendly   Sunlight friendly

Hardness: _____ Chakra: _____

Crystalline structure: _____

Country of origin: _____

MENTAL/EMOTIONAL PROPERTIES	PHYSICAL PROPERTIES	SPIRITUAL PROPERTIES

Intuitive vibe

_____

_____

_____

_____

Uses

_____

_____

_____

_____

_____

Notes

_____

_____

_____

_____

_____

Affirmation

_____

_____

_____

_____

Name: _____

Date of acquisition: _____

_____

Place: _____

_____

_____

*INSERT PICTURE OR
DRAWING OF YOUR CRYSTAL.*

Water friendly   Sunlight friendly

Hardness: _____ Chakra: _____

Crystalline structure: _____

Country of origin: _____

MENTAL/EMOTIONAL PROPERTIES	PHYSICAL PROPERTIES	SPIRITUAL PROPERTIES

Intuitive vibe

_____

_____

_____

_____

Uses

_____

_____

_____

_____

_____

Notes

_____

_____

_____

_____

_____

Affirmation

_____

_____

_____

_____

Name: _____

Date of acquisition: _____

_____

Place: _____

_____

_____

INSERT PICTURE OR DRAWING OF YOUR CRYSTAL.

Water friendly   Sunlight friendly

Hardness: _____ Chakra: _____

Crystalline structure: _____

Country of origin: _____

MENTAL/EMOTIONAL PROPERTIES	PHYSICAL PROPERTIES	SPIRITUAL PROPERTIES

Intuitive vibe

_____

_____

_____

_____

Uses

_____

_____

_____

_____

_____

Notes

_____

_____

_____

_____

_____

Affirmation

_____

_____

_____

_____

Name: _____

Date of acquisition: _____

_____

Place: _____

_____

*INSERT PICTURE OR
DRAWING OF YOUR CRYSTAL.*

_____

Water friendly   Sunlight friendly

Hardness: _____ Chakra: _____

Crystalline structure: _____

Country of origin: _____

MENTAL/EMOTIONAL PROPERTIES	PHYSICAL PROPERTIES	SPIRITUAL PROPERTIES

Intuitive vibe

_____

_____

_____

_____

Uses

_____

_____

_____

_____

Notes

_____

_____

_____

_____

Affirmation

_____

_____

_____

_____

Name: _____

Date of acquisition: _____

_____

Place: _____

_____

Water friendly   Sunlight friendly

Hardness: _____ Chakra: _____

Crystalline structure: _____

Country of origin: _____

MENTAL/EMOTIONAL PROPERTIES	PHYSICAL PROPERTIES	SPIRITUAL PROPERTIES

Intuitive vibe

_____

_____

_____

_____

Uses

_____

_____

_____

_____

_____

Notes

_____

_____

_____

_____

_____

Affirmation

_____

_____

_____

_____

Name: _____

Date of acquisition: _____

_____

Place: _____

_____

*INSERT PICTURE OR
DRAWING OF YOUR CRYSTAL.*

_____

Water friendly   Sunlight friendly

Hardness: _____ Chakra: _____

Crystalline structure: _____

Country of origin: _____

MENTAL/EMOTIONAL PROPERTIES	PHYSICAL PROPERTIES	SPIRITUAL PROPERTIES

Intuitive vibe

_____

_____

_____

_____

Uses

_____

_____

_____

_____

_____

Notes

_____

_____

_____

_____

_____

Affirmation

_____

_____

_____

_____

Name: _____

Date of acquisition: _____

_____

Place: _____

_____

_____

*INSERT PICTURE OR
DRAWING OF YOUR CRYSTAL.*

Water friendly   Sunlight friendly

Hardness: _____ Chakra: _____

Crystalline structure: _____

Country of origin: _____

MENTAL/EMOTIONAL PROPERTIES	PHYSICAL PROPERTIES	SPIRITUAL PROPERTIES

Intuitive vibe

_____

_____

_____

_____

Uses

_____

_____

_____

_____

_____

Notes

_____

_____

_____

_____

_____

Affirmation

_____

_____

_____

_____

Name: _____

Date of acquisition: _____

_____

Place: _____

_____

INSERT PICTURE OR
DRAWING OF YOUR CRYSTAL.

_____

Water friendly   Sunlight friendly

Hardness: _____ Chakra: _____

Crystalline structure: _____

Country of origin: _____

MENTAL/EMOTIONAL PROPERTIES	PHYSICAL PROPERTIES	SPIRITUAL PROPERTIES

Intuitive vibe

_____

_____

_____

_____

Uses

_____

_____

_____

_____

_____

Notes

_____

_____

_____

_____

_____

Affirmation

_____

_____

_____

_____

Name: _____

Date of acquisition: _____

_____

Place: _____

_____

*INSERT PICTURE OR
DRAWING OF YOUR CRYSTAL.*

_____

Water friendly   Sunlight friendly

Hardness: _____ Chakra: _____

Crystalline structure: _____

Country of origin: _____

MENTAL/EMOTIONAL PROPERTIES	PHYSICAL PROPERTIES	SPIRITUAL PROPERTIES

Intuitive vibe

_____

_____

_____

_____

Uses

_____

_____

_____

_____

_____

Notes

_____

_____

_____

_____

_____

Affirmation

_____

_____

_____

_____

Name: _____

Date of acquisition: _____

_____

Place: _____

_____

_____

*INSERT PICTURE OR
DRAWING OF YOUR CRYSTAL.*

Water friendly   Sunlight friendly

Hardness: _____ Chakra: _____

Crystalline structure: _____

Country of origin: _____

MENTAL/EMOTIONAL PROPERTIES	PHYSICAL PROPERTIES	SPIRITUAL PROPERTIES

Intuitive vibe

_____

_____

_____

_____

Uses

_____

_____

_____

_____

_____

Notes

_____

_____

_____

_____

_____

Affirmation

_____

_____

_____

_____

Name: _____

Date of acquisition: _____

_____

Place: _____

_____

*INSERT PICTURE OR
DRAWING OF YOUR CRYSTAL.*

_____

Water friendly   Sunlight friendly

Hardness: _____ Chakra: _____

Crystalline structure: _____

Country of origin: _____

MENTAL/EMOTIONAL PROPERTIES	PHYSICAL PROPERTIES	SPIRITUAL PROPERTIES

Intuitive vibe

_____

_____

_____

_____

Uses

_____

_____

_____

_____

_____

Notes

_____

_____

_____

_____

_____

Affirmation

_____

_____

_____

_____

Name: _____

Date of acquisition: _____

_____

Place: _____

_____

_____

*INSERT PICTURE OR
DRAWING OF YOUR CRYSTAL.*

Water friendly   Sunlight friendly

Hardness: _____ Chakra: _____

Crystalline structure: _____

Country of origin: _____

MENTAL/EMOTIONAL PROPERTIES	PHYSICAL PROPERTIES	SPIRITUAL PROPERTIES

Intuitive vibe

_____

_____

_____

_____

Uses

_____

_____

_____

_____

Notes

_____

_____

_____

_____

Affirmation

_____

_____

_____

_____

Name: _____

Date of acquisition: _____

_____

Place: _____

_____

INSERT PICTURE OR DRAWING OF YOUR CRYSTAL.

Water friendly   Sunlight friendly

Hardness: _____ Chakra: _____

Crystalline structure: _____

Country of origin: _____

MENTAL/EMOTIONAL PROPERTIES	PHYSICAL PROPERTIES	SPIRITUAL PROPERTIES

Intuitive vibe

_____

_____

_____

_____

Uses

_____

_____

_____

_____

_____

Notes

_____

_____

_____

_____

_____

Affirmation

_____

_____

_____

_____

Name: _____

Date of acquisition: _____

_____

Place: _____

_____

INSERT PICTURE OR
DRAWING OF YOUR CRYSTAL.

Water friendly   Sunlight friendly

Hardness: _____ Chakra: _____

Crystalline structure: _____

Country of origin: _____

MENTAL/EMOTIONAL PROPERTIES	PHYSICAL PROPERTIES	SPIRITUAL PROPERTIES

Intuitive vibe

_____

_____

_____

_____

Uses

_____

_____

_____

_____

_____

Notes

_____

_____

_____

_____

_____

Affirmation

_____

_____

_____

_____

Name: _____

Date of acquisition: _____

_____

Place: _____

_____

INSERT PICTURE OR DRAWING OF YOUR CRYSTAL.

Water friendly   Sunlight friendly

Hardness: _____ Chakra: _____

Crystalline structure: _____

Country of origin: _____

MENTAL/EMOTIONAL PROPERTIES	PHYSICAL PROPERTIES	SPIRITUAL PROPERTIES

Intuitive vibe

_____

_____

_____

_____

Uses

_____

_____

_____

_____

_____

Notes

_____

_____

_____

_____

_____

Affirmation

_____

_____

_____

_____

MY CRYSTAL WISH LIST

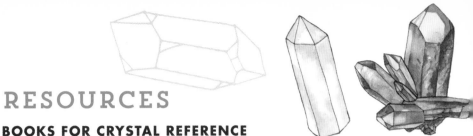

RESOURCES

BOOKS FOR CRYSTAL REFERENCE

Crystals by Jennie Harding: An awesome and extensive guide to crystals.

Gemstones of the World by Walter Schumann: A more technical approach if you love the nerdy stuff.

The Encyclopedia of Crystals by Judy Hall: Everything by Judy is amazing.

Add your own:

_____

_____

_____

BOOKS FOR WORKING WITH CRYSTALS

The Crystal Workshop by Azalea Lee: My favorite crystal book.

Crystal Enlightenment by Katrina Raphaell: An old book that is still so very relevant when it comes to crystal healing.

Crystal Grids by Henry M. Mason

Crystal Muse by Heather Askinosie and Timmi Jandro: Tons of rituals to do with crystals.

Add your own:

_____

_____

_____

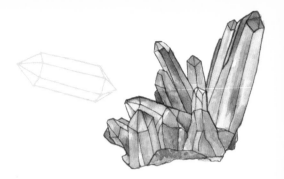

ON THE WEB

ORGANIC PUNK ROCKS
Instagram: @organicpunkrocks
Live sales on Instagram
Lizzy has crystals for the refined crystal collector looking for amazing rare finds.

MOONSTRUCK CRYSTALS
Instagram: @moonstruckcrystals
Live sales and story sales on Instagram
Best shop for sparkle and fun. If you like crystals shaped like coffins, moons, and full of druzy goodness, then Moonstruck is where you need to be.

LUNAR LOVE CRYSTALS
Instagram: @lunarlovecrystals
Live sales and feed sales on Instagram
Awesome selection of new and hip crystal finds.

ANCIENT MOUNTAIN TREASURES
Instagram: @ancientmountaintreasures
www.ancientmountaintreasures.com
Live sales, feed sales, and website
Huge diverse selection of crystals. They have a bit of everything for everybody.

BUSINESS NAME: _____

Web address: _____

Description: _____

BUSINESS NAME: _____

Web address: _____

Description: _____

CRYSTAL RESOURCES, PHYSICAL

BUSINESS NAME: _____

Address: _____

Phone/email: _____

Description: _____

_____

BUSINESS NAME: _____

Address: _____

Phone/email: _____

Description: _____

_____

BUSINESS NAME: _____

Address: _____

Phone/email: _____

Description: _____

_____

BUSINESS NAME: _____

Address: _____

Phone/email: _____

Description: _____

_____

NOTES

ABOUT THE AUTHOR

I am a soul who is dedicated to sharing mindful practices that help connect each of us back to our true authentic free spirit, so that we may live in an effortless, unlimited flow.

QUINN BOULEY

INSTAGRAM: @mindful_hookup
WEBSTORE: quinnbouley.com
YOUTUBE: Quinn Bouley